REAL life GUIDES

HOSPITALITY & EVENTS MANAGEMENT

ROSE MILLER & CAMILLA ZAJAC

trotman | t

10067097

Real Life Guide to Hospitality & Events Management

This first edition published in 2011 by Trotman, an imprint of
Crimson Publishing, Westminster House, Kew Road, Richmond
Surrey TW9 2ND

© Trotman Publishing 2011

Authors: Rose Miller & Camilla Zajac

British Library Cataloguing in Publication Data
A catalogue record for this book is available from the British
Library

ISBN: 978-1-84455-224-5

Typeset by IDSUK (DataConnection) Ltd
Printed and bound in the UK by Ashford Colour Press,
Gosport, Hants

CONTENTS

About the authors   vii

Acknowledgements   ix

Introduction   xi

Chapter 1   **Success story**   1

Chapter 2   **What is hospitality and events
             management?**   7

Chapter 3   **Real lives 1**   13

Chapter 4   **What are the jobs?**   17

Chapter 5   **Real lives 2**   31

Chapter 6   **Tools of the trade**   35

Chapter 7   **FAQs**   47

Chapter 8   **Real lives 3**   57

Chapter 9   **Training and qualifications**   61

Chapter 10   **The last word**   79

Chapter 11   **Further information**   83

ABOUT THE AUTHORS

ROSE MILLER

Rose Miller is a qualified careers guidance specialist and teacher, with over 20 years of experience in assisting young people and adults to make career decisions. She has written education-industry activities for schools and delivered a wide range of training activities to careers guidance professionals working in a range of locations, including colleges, Connexions, the voluntary sector and prisons. As well as being a freelance writer, she is currently employed by Warwick University as an open studies tutor and as an adult guidance worker at a further education college.

A graduate in English and Communication Studies from Liverpool University, she is currently studying for an MA in Literature, Politics and Identity at the University of Worcester.

CAMILLA ZAJAC

Camilla Zajac developed her role as a freelance careers writer whilst working in communications in the statutory and voluntary sector. She wrote for a wide range of careers resources aimed at young people, students and adults. Six years ago Camilla set up her own copywriting business and since then has written for communications and resources in the careers and business sectors. She lives and works in Nottingham.

ACKNOWLEDGEMENTS

The authors wish to thank the British Hospitality Association for its help and support.

INTRODUCTION

During the course of a week, it is guaranteed that most of us will experience the hospitality and food and beverage (often called 'catering') industry. Perhaps our packed lunches will contain bread from a supermarket bakery, or we will buy a snack from a canteen or café, whether at work, school or college. Perhaps at the weekend we might be lucky enough to be taken out for a meal in a pub, café or restaurant, or enjoy a short break in a hotel. A trip to the cinema, theatre, football ground, leisure park, fast food venue, concert hall, bowling alley or shopping complex is bound to bring us into contact with staff from hospitality and events management at some point.

Events management spans a wide range of promotional activities for a whole variety of industry sectors and is an incredibly useful strategic marketing and communication tool worth billions of pounds. It is a rapidly expanding industry in its own right, including events of all sizes from corporate business meetings to huge events such as the 2012 Olympic Games.

In Chapters 4, 5 and 6 of this book, real professionals from the hospitality and events management industry share their stories and offer you advice on starting your own career.

Let's take a look at what's coming up in the rest of the chapters.

▶ **Chapter 1: Success story.** For those aspiring chefs among you, read about Nathan Outlaw, a Michelin-starred chef who owns his own restaurant. His inspirational story will show you how you too can make a successful career for yourself as a chef.

▶ **Chapter 2: What is hospitality and events management?** This chapter will give you an overview of the whole sector, explaining what hospitality and events management really is, and how it has been affected by recent developments. It will also provide you with detailed information about the variety of sectors you could work in and how many people are already working in this industry.

▶ **Chapter 4: What are the jobs?** Chapter 4 looks more closely at the specific jobs in the sector and exactly what you could expect to do in your day-to-day work. This will give you a great insight into the industry and help you decide which jobs you're really interested in.

▶ **Chapter 6: Tools of the trade.** Find out what sort of skills and qualities you need in order to be successful in this career sector and how you can improve your skill set if you need to.

▶ **Chapter 7: FAQs.** Chapter 7 will answer the questions you really want to know, such as how much you'll get paid, whether you can work abroad and how your career can progress and take you to a more senior level.

▶ **Chapter 9: Training and qualifications.** Information on all the qualifications you can take that will set you up to enter the industry. This includes details on the 14–19 Diploma as well as Apprenticeships and NVQs.

▶ **Chapter 10: The last word.** By now you will have a great insight into this buzzing industry and will have decided if it's right for you. To make sure you're the right sort of person for the job, have a go at this light-hearted quiz and see if it's the right career choice for you!

▶ **Chapter 11: Further information.** Chapter 11 provides a long list of contacts where you can go to find more information about the sectors and start planning your exciting future career in hospitality and events management!

CHAPTER 1
SUCCESS STORY

Vital Stats: **Nathan Outlaw**

First job: Working in a golf club kitchen

Career high point: Being awarded a Michelin star for his successful restaurant

THE MICHELIN-STARRED CHEF

Nathan Outlaw manages food and beverage operations at the luxury, award-winning Marina Villa Hotel in Fowey, Cornwall. Restaurant Nathan Outlaw has been awarded a Michelin star, as well as a recommendation in *The Good Food Guide*. The restaurant offers two menus: the à la carte – which is five starters/mains/desserts and predominantly fish; and a seven-course tasting menu.

Nathan also manages his own restaurant at the St Enodoc Hotel in Rock, Cornwall, and has appeared on television programmes such as *Saturday Kitchen* (BBC1), *Great British Menu* (BBC2) and *The Market Kitchen* (UK TV Food). He is aware that in a rapidly changing industry, publicity is important to business success, and getting yourself known in the celebrity chef-dominated marketplace can have a positive impact.

> 66 In a rapidly changing industry, publicity is important to business success. 99

Nathan's dad is also a chef, so as a child Nathan was constantly around cooking and fresh food, and was also inspired to use fresh, local produce and simple ingredients by his grandparents, who kept a flourishing allotment.

His first job, working in a golf club kitchen, came about as a result of school work experience. He liked it because it offered a structured environment and 'proper rules'. He continued to work there part time and then left school to take a food preparation and cookery course at Thanet College in Broadstairs. Nathan's journey from his home in Maidstone to college every day took three hours. In this time he used to read books about food and do his homework. His catering course was well organised and enjoyable, and it included residential cookery placements in France. When he wasn't studying, he was still working at the golf club and at a pub over the weekends and throughout the holidays.

His last day at college was a Friday, and by the following Monday he was fully employed at the Hotel Inter-Continental in Hyde Park, London, working as a commis chef with 40 other chefs, gaining lots of ideas and support. He feels this was a better way to begin than working in a restaurant with split shifts. At the hotel he gained continuity and a professionally organised training environment. After a time, he obtained a long work experience stint at the restaurant of Gary Rhodes, moving on to the strict Gordon Ramsay-style catering environment managed by Eric Chavot. Nathan says, 'It's not a bad thing to have a year of really hard graft to get you focused – to really get into it.'

After this, Nathan worked as chef de partie in Rick Stein's fish restaurant in Padstow for two years. Then, moving area completely, he joined John Campbell (writer of *Practical Cookery*) as junior food chef at the Lords of the Manor Hotel in Upper Slaughter in the Cotswolds. The hotel was listed as one of the top 20 hotels in the country and, at the age of 21, Nathan took on the role of sous chef.

He believes that the way to get on in the industry is to keep putting yourself under pressure, so before long he was helping Rick Stein set up his new restaurant, Ripley's, in St Merryn, near Padstow. At this point his ideas were beginning to move towards self-employment, as he remembers wanting to know about the processes involved in setting up a small restaurant.

Nathan gained his first head chef job at the age of 23, re-joining John Campbell, now at the Vineyard at Stockcross in Berkshire. He was in charge of a kitchen with 22 chefs and remembers that effective communication was an important challenge: 'Some of the chefs were quite a lot older than me, and not all were native English speakers.'

Nathan's wife comes from Cornwall and they decided to move back to her home area to start a family. He opened the Black Pig restaurant at Rock in 2003, and within eight months the restaurant had gained a Michelin star. He was owner/chef in a four-person team. 'I still feel that if you're starting your own business, you should begin with something small, and then go for something bigger when you have experience.'

Wanting to take his food in a different direction, Nathan sold his restaurant within three years and began work at St Ervan Manor, near Padstow, with 20 covers (place settings in a restaurant). But when the owner wanted to move to London, Nathan had a decision to make. It was then that the Marina Villa Hotel invited him to take over its whole food and beverage service, and he was able to give his own name to the restaurant! Three months ago Nathan opened his second restaurant, Nathan Outlaw's Sea Food and Grill, at the St Enodoc Hotel. Here, customers can enjoy views across the estuary while dining al fresco.

Nathan's career has been as focused and fast-paced as the industry he works in. As he says, 'The only way to get on is through hard work.'

A typical day begins at 6.30am. He always prepares breakfast for his children, who are 6 and 4 years old. 'This is my chance to spend some time with them before beginning work,' he says. Usually, he travels to the restaurant in Rock to check that the staff are ok. 'This includes supporting and gaining feedback from the hotel staff as well as the kitchen staff, as we both deal with the same customers.' He checks the accounts, and by midday he is on his way to the Marina Villa Hotel where he is in charge of the lunch service. In the afternoon he typically completes administrative tasks and works on venue development. This is followed by meat preparation in the kitchen. By 7pm, preparation has to be completed for 38–40 covers in the restaurant. He will work until about 11.30pm, returning home at about midnight.

'As we are in a tourist area, summer is the busiest time, for about 12 weeks, and I am currently thinking of ways to extend the season. My advice to new chefs would be to ensure that you are organised in everything you do, and learn how to delegate, as you cannot possibly do everything.'

As a chef, Nathan prefers working with local suppliers dedicated to great produce. 'I only hope I can do justice to these fantastic products in my restaurant . . . when it comes to writing a menu I start with the flavours and work back.' In the provision of wine for his guests, he focuses on suppliers who use organic farming methods.

Nathan says that his main frustration with the job is the hours he works, which intrude on his time with his family. When he does have spare time, he likes to spend it with his wife and children, sea fishing, and supporting Chelsea Football Club.

'Another frustration is that there are not enough well-trained young adults who want to come into the industry. A common mistake is expecting quick, celebrity status, like Jamie Oliver, whereas the reality can be doing the washing up because you're short staffed in the kitchen.

> **66** It's not a bad thing to have a year of really hard graft to get you focused – to really get into it. **99**

'It would be useful if there were specialist training courses for the talented, extra-motivated few who are serious about becoming professional chefs. The extra focus and support would provide the impetus to continue and succeed in the industry. The "15" project is a great idea, as it involves working with students who have been hand picked, who want to do well.'

Reflecting on his career and achievements so far and asked what he is most proud of, Nathan smiles and replies: 'The staff that I've trained and who have gone on to do well in other restaurants.'

Nathan's top tip
66 To get on in the industry, keep putting yourself under pressure. 99

CHAPTER 2
WHAT IS HOSPITALITY AND EVENTS MANAGEMENT?

Hospitality and events management is a broad industry that covers many different activities, but what they all have in common is providing services to make people feel welcome, comfortable and allow them to have an enjoyable experience.

Have you dropped into a local café recently or had a quick coffee at your local leisure centre? Perhaps you've stayed somewhere for the weekend or attended a music festival. From business to leisure and from the professional to the personal, hospitality and events management touches on many areas of everyday life.

You only need to look around your local high street to see the variety of outlets and businesses the sector covers, from small businesses such as cafés to major hotel chains. It ranges from regular activities such as

> ## ⚡ NEWSFLASH!
> The hospitality, leisure, travel and tourism industry employs more than 1.9m people.
> *Source: British Hospitality Association (BHA).*

eating meals and attending training events to more leisurely interests such as going on holiday or attending a public sports event.

WHAT'S THE WORK LIKE?

As you would expect with a sector that provides services to people, this is a fast-moving and physically demanding area to work in. As you might imagine, having a job in a restaurant, pub or hotel often means working long and unsociable hours. Dealing with people demands a sociable nature and a friendly, professional approach. You will also need to be quick on your feet and have plenty of stamina.

A GREAT VARIETY OF JOBS

 **NEWSFLASH!**

The *Michelin Guide* was created in 1900 by André Michelin, part of the team behind the car products company that produces Michelin tyres. It awards one to three stars to restaurants of outstanding quality. Its guidelines for awarding stars are:

► one star: 'a good restaurant or pub in its category'
► two stars: 'excellent cooking'
► three stars: 'exceptional cuisine'.

Working in hospitality doesn't just mean having a job in a large hotel, and events management isn't purely about organising meetings. In hospitality you could be involved with taking care of guests in an independent guest house – or you could set up your own specialist catering business. In events management, you could provide support at one-off events or help to put together themed weekends in cities around the world. As you will see, there's much more to this industry than meets the eye.

A VARIED INDUSTRY

Hospitality and events management includes many different areas and organisations, as listed below.

Sector	What does it involve?
Catering	Catering involves providing food services in a range of settings such as businesses, schools, hospitals and retail outlets. This includes preparing and serving food and managing the venue.
Contract catering	Contract catering means catering services that are contracted out or provided by an outside company. There are a range of companies dedicated to providing catering services in places such as universities and department stores.
Facilities management	Managing and maintaining buildings or facilities such as office suites and residential homes.
Bar and pub management and work	Pub companies and independent pubs need people to run and staff them. The kinds of places you could work in vary widely.
Restaurant and café management and work	Look around and you'll notice all kinds of places to eat – from fast food outlets to fine dining. All of them need staff to keep them running smoothly.
Hotels	Whether it's an overnight stay for work or a special holiday visit, there are hotel chains, independent hotels and B&Bs of all kinds across the UK. They all need staff to run and maintain them, manage reservations and provide waiting and bar service.
Events management: corporate	Events management involves developing, organising and managing events such as product launches, awards ceremonies, corporate hospitality, charity events conferences and staff training days. This can be done in house or by one of the growing number of dedicated events management companies.

Sector	What does it involve?
Events management: private	There is more and more demand for private events management services. This involves planning and managing events such as weddings, hen parties and birthday parties.

IS IT A THRIVING INDUSTRY?

Both the hospitality and events management industries are huge and they have grown a great deal over the past few years. For example, the exhibitions industry alone has been found to support 137,000 jobs and contribute £9.3bn to the UK economy. (Source: Association of Exhibition Organisers (AEO).)

Pubs serving food have been found to be doing well because more people are choosing to visit pubs to eat as well as to drink. (Source: Caterersearch.)

One particularly strong area of the hospitality sector is hotels. For example:

- ▶ 150 new hotels are being built every year in the UK
- ▶ the budget hotel sector, with nearly 6,000 rooms opening in 2009, has the biggest share
- ▶ in 2001, there were 50,000 budget hotel rooms – this figure increased to 105,000 in 2009
- ▶ a total of 11,000 new hotel rooms opened in 2009 and a further 40,000 are to be created between 2010 and 2015.

The recession in 2009 has actually led to some positive changes for the industry. For example, more British people are trying to save money by taking a holiday here in the UK rather than going abroad. This is good news for hotels, restaurants and visitor attractions in the UK and it's a trend that looks set to continue. According to a poll commissioned by tourist board VisitEngland and undertaken in 2009, almost three-quarters of UK consumers said they were planning to take a holiday in England in 2010. Out of more than 1,000 UK residents, 72% said they were likely to take a break in England in 2010.

This is great news because it will create hundreds of new and exciting jobs and great opportunities for people entering the sector.

WHAT ARE THE WORKERS LIKE?

Hospitality is a young industry, especially at junior levels. In fact 47% of employees are aged under 30 years old and 15% are under 20. Just 18% of employees are aged over 50 (Source: British Hospitality Association (BHA) *2009 Trends Report.*) While at more junior levels the mix of male and female employees is fairly balanced, the industry is male-dominated at management level.

Staff turnover is generally higher in hospitality than in many other industries. (Source: BHA *2009 Trends Report*.) The seasonal aspect of the industry is one reason for this. Another is that the industry offers temporary opportunities that suit

⚡ NEWSFLASH!
In 2010, Britain's pubs were closing at a rate of 30 per week.

people with other commitments, such as students.

THE FUTURE OF HOSPITALITY AND EVENTS MANAGEMENT

Companies across the sector are positive about the future and what it holds for them and their employees. In spite of the economic recession in 2009, the number of employees in the three principal sectors of the industry – hotels, restaurants and pubs – is rising. (Source: BHA.) While the number of people working in and managing bars and pubs has fallen, other areas have grown. For example, there was a 27% increase in the number of people working as conference and exhibition managers between 2003 and 2008 and a 13% increase in the number of people working as hotel and accommodation managers over the same period. (Source: People 1st).

High-profile sporting events are expected to boost the leisure and hospitality sector in the future. Events such as the 2012 Olympic Games, the 2014 Commonwealth Games and the 2015 Rugby World Cup should help to increase employment opportunities in the sector over the next decade. The government wants to create 200,000 more jobs in the sector by 2017; 69,000 of these should be management roles.

Quick recap!
✓ Hospitality and events management is a growing sector, which means there are new jobs being created all the time.
✓ This is a young industry so you will be working with people of a similar sort of age to you.
✓ You can find jobs in this sector in a huge variety of places, no matter what your interest, be it organising music events, working in catering, being the friendly face customers see when entering a hotel or the person whipping up delicious food in a restaurant kitchen!

CHAPTER 3
REAL LIVES 1

GAIL MEADS: HOUSEKEEPER/FE LECTURER

When Gail left school after doing her A levels she went to London and initially trained as a beauty therapist. She has always worked in a service industry and enjoys working with people.

'My first experience of working within the hospitality industry was when I was starting up as a mobile beauty therapist in my early 20s and needed to supplement my income. I worked as a receptionist in a small local hotel working four evenings a week and enjoyed the variety of the job. Although I worked in the reception area I gained valuable experience in all areas of the hotel and enjoyed all areas of customer service.'

Over the years Gail has worked in a number of different service-related industries and when, after having children, she needed to earn a few extra pennies and take some time out from full-time motherhood, she found a job in a nearby hotel.

> 66 Being responsible for the smooth running of the hotel, I learned to deal with many situations and to be calm and level headed. 99

'With all the experience I had in the previous hotel, my silver service skills secured me the job. I started working two nights a week in a waiting role and then progressed to supervising the restaurant on quiet Sunday nights.

'When the children went to school I started working during the day and on occasion was left in charge. I took on more responsibility, overseeing a number of staff, monitoring wages, stocktaking and ordering wines and spirits. I then gradually started taking over all the staff training and customer service training, also becoming duty manager in the evening. Being responsible for the smooth running of the hotel, I learned to deal with many situations and to be calm and level headed. Dealing with customers has given me valuable experience.'

In 2000, Gail was offered the job of restaurant manager in the Hanover International Hotel, with responsibility for running a 100-seater restaurant, and supervisory responsibility for three supervisors and 20 other staff. She didn't accept it straight away. Her main concern was that she was not qualified to do the job. The only qualification she had was the food hygiene certificate that was delivered by the company and was compulsory. She was eventually persuaded that although she had no direct qualifications, the experience she had gained over the past six years would enable her to do the job. She went on to run the restaurant for four successful years and the only reason she gave it up was because of family commitments. She continued working part time in restaurant management at an alternative hotel.

'Working in the hospitality industry is not a Monday to Friday, nine-to-five job. You have to be on standby if there is an emergency. This can range from an unexpected number of people staying at the hotel (which happened when the motorway was closed due to a severe snowstorm and people were brought to the hotel by the rescue services), to staff not turning up for work.'

After Gail left the hotel, she began working part time in customer services at the local college.

'Working in the college has made me realise that I should have looked into training within the hotel and local colleges during my time there. You have to make the effort yourself. I am fortunate in that working in the college I now know what is available, but it is knowing where to look.'

Since working at North East Worcestershire College, Gail has taken her NVQ level 3 (Supervisory) in Hospitality and Catering and a Certificate in Teaching in the Lifelong Learning Sector, which now enables her to teach in the college's hospitality department. She is now an associate lecturer.

'I teach "front of house" and customer service. I am now about to embark on a Higher National Certificate (HNC) course in Hospitality and Management.'

Gail's top tip
❝ I would recommend working in the hospitality area if you enjoy working with people, don't mind working hard and are able to react quickly to difficult situations. The career is very rewarding and develops personnel skills, customer service skills and promotes good team working. This applies to all areas, from working in the restaurant as a waiter to supervising, to management level. ❞

CHAPTER 4
WHAT ARE THE JOBS?

There are many different jobs available in this industry. From taking care of a company's big product launch as an events organiser to making a new customer feel at home in your hotel

> 66 Your choice of employer is as important as the job you choose. 99

as a hotel receptionist, you'll find there are opportunities to suit all kinds of people.

This is a flexible industry, so there are opportunities to work part time whilst studying or managing other commitments. However, this flexibility also means that opportunities can be temporary, seasonal or short term, without the chance to gain further qualifications.

Your choice of employer is as important as the job you choose. Larger or more established employers may be more likely to offer training and development schemes. In some areas of this industry it is possible to start at entry level without qualifications and work your way up to more senior roles, gaining further qualifications along the way. You'll learn more about training and qualifications in Chapter 9.

BARS AND PUBS

This sector varies widely, from country pubs to packed-out city bars. It can be a sociable and fast-moving setting to work in, but it's very physically demanding, too. Being on your feet a lot of the time and working weekends and late nights can be tough.

Bar person

As a bar person you would have an important role in providing great customer service to keep the customers happy. Your job also involves working to strict health and safety regulations. The minimum age at which you can work in a bar is usually 18 years old.

Your job would involve:

▶ keeping the bar area clean, tidy and welcoming

▶ serving drinks and snacks to customers

▶ taking payments and handling cash.

What could I earn?
Salaries range from £10,000 to £17,000.

Bar manager/publican/licensee

You would be responsible for managing a pub or bar which is licensed to sell alcohol. This could be a bar that is part of a chain, or your own pub. This is a varied job, which demands the ability to manage people, work well with customers, take care of stock and make sure your venue is up to date with strict licensing regulations. Your accommodation might be provided as part of your pay and benefits package.

Your job would involve:

- ▶ recruiting, training and managing staff
- ▶ making sure that the venue meets all the relevant licensing and health and safety regulations
- ▶ managing and maintaining stocks of drinks and food
- ▶ managing the accounts and the business development of the venue.

What could I earn?

As a trainee manager you could earn from £12,000 to £15,000. With more experience, you could go on to earn £20,000–£40,000.

Bar/pub food service

Food is big business in pubs. Food service could form part of your bar duties or you could work as waiting staff in a dedicated dining/restaurant area of the pub or bar. Either way, it is likely that your work activities would include:

> ⚡ **NEWSFLASH!**
>
> The term 'pub' comes from 'public house', a term invented by the Victorians. The Romans brought the first pubs to England almost 2,000 years ago.

- ▶ setting up and preparing the dining area
- ▶ taking orders and payments for food
- ▶ taking orders to the table
- ▶ clearing plates after customers have had their meal.

What could I earn?

It is likely that you would be paid at a similar level to a bar person. In some venues you may also receive tips from customers.

HOTELS AND ACCOMMODATION

The future is looking good for the hotel and accommodation sector. The UK hotel sector employs more than 222,000 people in establishments ranging from country houses to exclusive hotels in central London. In spite of the recent recession, plans are moving ahead for developing new hotels, particularly in the budget sector.

Hotel porter

You would be part of the team on hand to make guests feel welcome. You're one of the first people they meet, so you need to create a great first impression.

Your job would involve:

- showing guests to their rooms and helping them with their luggage
- taking and passing on messages to guests
- dealing with enquiries and making room reservations
- undertaking additional tasks as and when they need doing, for example collecting dry cleaning. .

What could I earn?
You could earn from £12,000 to £24,000 a year.

 **NEWSFLASH!**

There was a 13% increase in the number of people working as hotel and accommodation managers between 2003 and 2008.

Receptionist

Like the idea of being the public face of an organisation? In this job you would be one of the first people guests have contact with. You'll be in the front line of everyday hotel life and will be expected to respond to issues and enquiries that arise, as well as managing your regular duties.

Your job would involve:

- ▶ handling calls, taking room bookings and passing on messages
- ▶ helping guests book in and out of their rooms
- ▶ answering queries and providing information as and when guests need it
- ▶ dealing with issues such as lost property and customer complaints.

What could I earn?
Starting salaries begin at around £12,000 and at senior levels can increase to £25,000.

Hotel manager

The success of the hotel rests with you, whether you're in charge of an exclusive city centre boutique hotel or managing a budget hotel which is part of a chain. It's your job to take care of guests, staff, supplies and setting, to ensure your hotel stays well looked after and booked up.

> 66 Like the idea of being the public face of an organisation? As a receptionist you would be one of the first people guests have contact with. 99

Your job would involve:

- ▶ setting and managing the hotel budget in areas such as staffing, stock and maintenance
- ▶ recruiting, training and managing staff
- ▶ developing and/or working to a marketing strategy for the hotel

► making sure the hotel meets all the relevant health and safety legislation.

What could I earn?

Your earnings would depend on the size and style of hotel you manage. Starting salaries begin at around £17,000 and with experience, can increase to as much as £60,000 in larger hotels.

Room attendant

A clean, welcoming room is an essential part of a stay in any hotel, B&B or guesthouse. In this role you would have an important part in creating a positive impression and maintaining the health and safety of each room.

Your job would involve:

► making beds and changing bed linen
► cleaning and tidying the rooms and guest bathrooms
► emptying bins
► restocking supplies such as soap, towels, tea and coffee.

What could I earn?

You could earn from £8,000 up to £15,000 a year. You might also receive tips from guests.

FOOD SERVICE/RESTAURANTS

Food service professionals work in all kinds of places – from fast food outlets to small independent cafés. All these venues need people to run and staff them. Food and food service is the hospitality industry's main activity, even during more difficult economic times. The restaurant sector is the largest in terms of employment, with a total of 567,600 people. In fact, chefs and kitchen staff account for almost one-third of all hospitality employment, with waiters and restaurant managers making up a further 19%.

 **NEWSFLASH!**

The restaurant sector is the largest in terms of employment in the hospitality industry, with a total of 567,600 people.

Chef

If the customers don't like the food, they won't come back! Chefs play an important part in the success of any food service business. They have to maintain a high standard of work night after night, often working under great pressure in a busy kitchen environment. There is currently a high demand for chefs among employers. It is the role that employers in this sector find most difficult to recruit for, mainly due to a lack of applicants with the required skills. It may also be due to the fact that more businesses are employing chefs than before. For example, many pubs have introduced food in a response to the smoking ban and falling drink sales.

Your job would involve:

- ▶ preparing and creating dishes from fresh ingredients
- ▶ planning and budgeting for future food service
- ▶ overseeing and managing other kitchen staff
- ▶ maintaining health and safety guidelines in the kitchen.

What could I earn?

As a commis (trainee) chef you could earn £12,000 a year. With experience this could increase from £15,000 to

> 66 There is currently a high demand for chefs among employers. 99

£30,000. You may be able to earn more than this as the head chef in a major hotel.

Catering/restaurant manager

In this job you would be the person responsible for the smooth running of the restaurant or food outlet. You might be in charge of your own independent restaurant, or the manager of one of a chain of food outlets. Either way, you have an important role in the success of the business.

Your job would involve:

- ▶ recruiting, training and managing staff
- ▶ planning the menu
- ▶ overseeing the budget for staffing, food and supplies
- ▶ making sure the restaurant or venue meets all relevant health and safety legislation.

What could I earn?

In a trainee role you could earn from £14,000 to £20,000 a year. With experience you could be paid up to £65,000 a year.

Waiting staff

In this job, customer service is everything. After all, you're the person bringing the guests their food and drinks. Your approach will help ensure that the guests feel welcome and want to return.

Your job would involve:

- ▶ welcoming customers, showing them to their table and taking their orders for food and drink
- ▶ bringing customers their food

▶ taking payments at the end of the meal

▶ clearing away plates and setting tables.

What could I earn?

As a new starter you could earn £8,000–£11,000. With experience you could earn £12,000–£15,000 and as a head waiter or waitress you could earn up to £20,000. Depending on the type of venue you work in, you may also receive tips from customers.

> 66 Your approach will help ensure that the guests feel welcome and want to return. 99

Kitchen assistant/porter

The kitchen assistant is a key part of keeping the kitchen and the food service running smoothly. Their duties ensure that the chef and kitchen staff have the supplies and tools ready to do their job.

Your job would involve:

▶ setting up the kitchen before cooking and service starts and cleaning it afterwards

▶ unpacking and storing food when it is delivered by suppliers

▶ preparing food for cooking

▶ cleaning and preparing kitchen equipment.

What could I earn?

As a new starter you could earn about £8,000. With more experience you could earn £9,000, which could increase up to £16,000.

EVENTS MANAGEMENT

Events management is a growing area of the hospitality sector. The number of people working as conference and exhibition managers grew by 27% between 2003 and 2008. Large organisations rely on events professionals to put together events for training, promotion and sales. Trade fairs, conferences and exhibitions are now high-profile affairs that call for professionals to help make them a success. Moving from the public and professional to the extra special, events organisers also plan and organise occasions such as wedding parties and birthday celebrations.

Events manager/organiser

You could be involved with arranging an exclusive party or putting together a staff training day. Whatever the nature of the event, you'll need to make sure it all comes together at the right time – guests, venue, entertainment, security and more. You could work in house for a business or for one of the many professional events management companies out there, or even run your own events business. The nature of the job would mean long hours on your feet and weekend and evening working.

Your job would involve:

▶ developing, planning and putting on events to meet the requirements of your employer or client. These could be exhibitions, product launches or private social events

▶ organising venues, guest lists and bookings for events

▶ arranging additional aspects such as lighting, music and props

▶ attending events to make sure they run smoothly.

What could I earn?

Salary levels would depend on the type of organisation you work for, or whether you are self-employed. Salaries range from £19,000 to £24,000, increasing to £25,000–£45,000 with more experience.

> 66 Whatever the nature of the event, you'll need to make sure it all comes together at the right time – guests, venue, entertainment, security and more. 99

Entertainment/functions manager

You're the one who makes sure the event goes without a hitch and meets your customers' expectations. You could be employed by a hotel, a restaurant or a large company, or you could work for yourself. You could be working in one venue or planning events in a range of locations, including outdoors. The nature of the job means you would work late nights and probably weekends.

Your job would involve:

- ▶ planning and preparing for events such as wedding receptions, birthday parties, discos and social events
- ▶ setting up and preparing the venue for the event
- ▶ managing and overseeing staff and suppliers involved with the event, such as waiting staff and entertainers
- ▶ managing the team that clears up after the event.

What could I earn?

You could earn from £13,000 to £20,000 a year, depending on your level of experience. This could increase to £30,000.

Wedding planner/consultant

In this role you're planning and managing what, for many people, is the biggest day of their lives. It's important to get it right! This calls for exceptional organisational skills and great attention to detail. You could work for yourself or for a dedicated wedding and events management company.

Your job would involve:

► agreeing with your customers what they want from their wedding and agreeing a budget

► developing ideas for a wedding theme or style

► booking and organising the wedding and wedding reception venue

► arranging suppliers such as caterers, florists and musicians.

What could I earn?
Working for a company, you would start at around £15,000–£18,000. With experience, this would increase to £22,000–£40,000. As a freelance wedding planner you would either charge an agreed overall rate or a percentage of the total cost of the wedding.

WHAT'S NEXT?

As you can see, this sector offers many types of jobs in a variety of settings. They may be different, but they all require a great mix of customer service and hands-on skills. You'll find out more about the skills you need to work in this sector in Chapter 6, 'Tools of the Trade'.

Quick recap!

✓ In this industry, tips can make a lot of difference to your wages.
✓ For almost all the jobs in this sector, attention to detail is vital.
✓ There are many senior roles you can progress to if you're willing to work hard.

CHAPTER 5
REAL LIVES 2

ABI HUMAYUN: CO-FOUNDER, RAPPORT EVENTS

After studying European Studies and Spanish at the University of Manchester (which included a year spent living and studying in Barcelona), Abi graduated in 2001 with a 2.1 BA Hons degree. As she was unsure of her path, she decided to get a temp job in the human resources department of the Co-operative Insurance company to test out the possibility of a career in HR. However, she quickly realised that HR was not for her and became convinced that a career in events was her ultimate goal.

'After nine months of applying for events jobs around the country, I was fortunate to be offered a role as an events co-ordinator at a technical production company based in south Manchester. Even though technical production was not the area of events that I was most interested in, I realised that it was an invaluable foot in the door to advance my career. The experience I gained from working at this company was second to none; I learned invaluable project management skills and developed an awareness of technical production that even surprised myself.'

Abi's career within this company developed and she was promoted to events manager, a position that she held for three years. However, she had a real desire to explore different avenues of events and to offer a service that wasn't reliant on technical production. This resulted in her leaving the company in March 2007 to set up Rapport Events along with her business partner.

'Initially things were hard work. Neither of us had experience of running our own company and we had to learn fast, on the job. We got our first event booked in within three weeks of setting up the business, which was fantastic but very hard work, as we had no real processes set up.

'We successfully delivered our first couple of events and started developing processes that would set us in good stead to handle more business, like establishing a dedicated budget system database to help us compile costs electronically rather than manually calculating costs and profit. We also looked at recruiting our first team member and decided to move offices to be in a more central location to attract talent (our first office had been cheap and functional but not desirable and was located quite far outside the city centre).'

Eight months after setting up Rapport, the business was going from strength to strength and Abi and her colleague were delivering events across the world but still with limited internal resources. They therefore made the decision to recruit two more team members: another events assistant and a graphic designer.

'With the extra team members on board my business partner and I were able to focus on developing our service to ensure that we were offering something that our clients would really focus on. We knew we had a strong name in Rapport so we decided to further develop our offering around this and focusing on helping our clients to build rapport with their audiences through event-led communication.'

> 66 In this day and age, events are no longer about just having fun . . . companies are having to focus more on the content and outcomes of their event. 99

On a day-to-day basis Abi helps clients develop events that meet their business and motivational objectives and the aim is to ensure that return on investment is calculated for a proportion of these.

'In this day and age, events are no longer about just having fun – in order to justify event budgets companies are having to focus more on the content and outcomes of their event, namely learning and the application of learning post-meeting.'

As an events manager, Abi finds that no two days are the same. A role working in events can cover many areas: logistics and delegate management, production and audiovisual displays, creative theming, content management and providing architecture.

Reflecting on the skills required for a successful career in events, Abi states that these would be: 'Great communication skills, ability to multitask, thoroughness and high attention to detail, ability to remain calm under pressure, ability to think on your feet, fantastic people skills to effectively deal with suppliers and clients, be highly professional, IT proficient, and have an understanding of budget management and good administration skills.

'I would also say that anyone considering a career in events needs to be comfortable travelling to events and being away from home a lot. The days working on site at events are long, hard and can be physically and mentally draining; however, they are also a lot of fun and if you are the type of person to thrive on adrenaline and think you have the attributes listed above, a career in events could be for you!'

Abi's top tip

66 Great communication skills, ability to multitask, thoroughness and high attention to detail, ability to remain calm and fantastic people skills are all vital in events management. 99

CHAPTER 6
TOOLS OF THE TRADE

Any member of staff coming into contact with the customer is also part of the product. No matter how good the quality of the food, beverage, décor and equipment, poorly trained, scruffy or unhelpful staff can destroy a customer's potential satisfaction. It is also true that well-trained, smart and helpful staff can sometimes make up for aspects that are lacking elsewhere.

These current and future skills needs in the hospitality sector and sub-sectors are all transferable to events management and conference and exhibition organising.

WILLINGNESS TO LEARN

Being willing to learn new knowledge and skills not only creates a good impression with any employer, but also shows that you are motivated and keen to progress, both within a company and in your career. In an industry which constantly changes and adapts to suit customers' spending habits and needs, it is important to be flexible and adaptable yourself.

> 66 In an industry which constantly changes and adapts to suit customers' spending habits and needs, it is important to be flexible and adaptable yourself. 99

Transferable skills and qualities such as teamwork, communication skills, personal presentation and customer service, general fitness and stamina, punctuality, honesty (in fact most of the skills and qualities listed below), are needed in most forms of employment, but jobs will also have specific duties and technical skills and competencies, which you will also need to learn, in order to move ahead in your career, or even to just keep pace with change.

PERSONAL PRESENTATION

Staff should be clean and well-presented. In food preparation and front-of-house roles, particular attention should be paid to the hands and men should normally be clean shaven or with any moustache or beard neatly trimmed. Women should wear only light make-up. In restaurant and food preparation work, earrings should not be worn (with the possible exception of studs/sleepers). Uniforms should be clean, starched as appropriate and neatly pressed, with all buttons present. Hair must be clean and well groomed and long hair must be tied up at the back to prevent it falling into food and drinks, and to avoid repeated handling of the hair. Shoes must be comfortable and clean, and of a plain, neat design; fashion is not as important as safety and foot comfort.

> **"** In events management, conference and exhibition organising, creating a positive and efficient initial impression is very important when working face to face with clients. **"**

In events management, conference and exhibition organising, creating a positive and efficient initial impression is very important when working face to face with clients and visitors, particularly in sales and marketing roles, management and public relations.

FITNESS

Sufficient sleep, an adequate and healthy intake of food and regular exercise are essential for good health and the ability to cope with the pressures and stress of work. Remember, some work is physically tiring, involving working shifts and being on your feet for long periods (such as waiting, working behind a bar). You need stamina to cook in a hot atmosphere, move luggage if you are a porter, and clean hotel rooms. Checking that everything is running smoothly during an event, or trying to sort out a problem on the day, also requires energy and stamina.

PUNCTUALITY

Punctuality is all-important. If staff are continually late on duty it shows a lack of interest in their work and a lack of respect for the management and customers.

TOP TIP!
Punctuality is all-important.

INITIATIVE

Sometimes you will be expected to make quick, on-the-spot decisions to solve a problem or deal with a situation. This is where common sense, the ability to think independently and using your own initiative will come in handy. If you have had good training, and are familiar with company procedures and policies, you will be prepared and know what to do. If you are unsure, there will be someone who will know the answer, or the best way of dealing with an issue, and you can always ask someone else on the staff who may have more experience, such as a manager, supervisor or mentor.

ABILITY TO FOLLOW INSTRUCTIONS

Receiving good training and thorough preparation will help you to know what to do when someone gives you an order or instruction. It is important to listen and attend carefully. During your induction into a company, ensure you read the necessary information so that you can find your way around quickly and get to know who's who within the company structure, so that if you have to act quickly, for example in an emergency, you do not waste precious time.

 NEWSFLASH!

Over 14% of all people working within the hospitality sector are self-employed.

EXPLODE THAT MYTH!
If your memory isn't great, you're not going to be able to get a job in this sector

It's really important that you are able to follow instructions in this industry, especially when it comes to keeping yourself and others safe. However, there's no harm in asking questions if you can't take in all the information you're given at once. Keep a notepad with you to jot things down. You'll soon get the hang of how everything works once you've done the job a few times.

This is where having a good memory will come in useful. Write notes in a notebook if you don't think you can keep everything in your head at once. However, if you do forget, ask someone to repeat an instruction. This is better than neglecting to do something or making lots of errors. Don't forget that everyone has been 'the new employee' at some point in their career and will understand and remember how confusing joining a new organisation can be.

If you are in an organisational or management role, you will need to give instructions clearly and concisely, and ensure that your instructions are carried out quickly and efficiently. A certain amount of tact is needed when giving instructions, as the manner in which you ask for something to be done can affect the task in hand, and the motivation of the staff involved.

LOCAL KNOWLEDGE

The staff should have a certain knowledge of the area in which they work so that they can advise the guests about the various forms of entertainment offered, the best means of transport to places of interest, and so on.

COMMUNICATION SKILLS

You will need to be tactful, courteous, good humoured and even tempered. You must converse with the customer in a pleasant and well-spoken manner, and the ability to smile at the right time pays dividends. A good memory is an asset to food and beverage service staff. It may help in various ways in your work if you know the likes and dislikes of customers, where they like to sit in the food service area, what their favourite drinks are, and so on.

TOP TIP!

It may help in various ways in your work if you know the likes and dislikes of customers, where they like to sit in the food service area, what their favourite drinks are, and so on.

The Association of Exhibition Organisers lists the ability to communicate at all levels as an essential quality, plus assertiveness and the ability to develop relationships with industry publications staff and associations. In sales roles, you will need determination, tenacity, resilience, a professional attitude and a high level of self-motivation. In operations and logistics roles, you need experience of managing others, in order to deal effectively with contractors, and good negotiation skills.

HONESTY

This is all-important for staff in their dealings with both customers and management. If there is trust and respect in the triangle of staff, customer and management relationships, there will be an atmosphere that encourages efficiency and a good team spirit. Loyalty and integrity are important qualities across the hospitality, food and beverages and events management sectors. Your conduct must be impeccable, especially in front of customers. The rules and regulations of an establishment must be followed and respect shown to all senior members of staff.

> 66 Your conduct must be impeccable, especially in front of customers. 99

JOB-SPECIFIC SKILLS

In some food and beverage roles, you must have sufficient knowledge of all the items on the menu and wine and drink lists in order to advise and offer suggestions to customers. In addition, you must know how to serve each dish on the menu correctly, what its accompaniments are, the correct cover, and the make-up of the dish and its garnish. For beverage service you should know how to serve various types of wine and drink, in the correct containers (e.g. glasses, cups) and at the right temperature.

In events management, conferences and exhibition organising, sales professionals are the dynamic centre of an exhibition company, contributing the most to revenue through stand sales, sponsorship, etc. In addition to excellent presentation skills, both over the telephone and face to face, the sales function includes researching markets, identifying potential exhibitors and sponsors within that market and selling the concept of the show.

In operations roles, all events have to be organised efficiently, safely and within tight time and budget constraints, meeting all requirements and paying close attention to detail. In a marketing role, you would need good planning and prioritising skills, creativity, direct mail experience, the ability to understand and research market sectors and experience of managing and negotiating with different agencies and suppliers.

The staff reflect the image of the establishment. They are salespeople and must therefore have a complete knowledge of all forms of food and drink and their correct service, and so be able to contribute to personal selling and merchandising. In order for the establishment to generate the maximum amount of business over the service period, with as high a net profit as possible, staff must develop a sense of urgency.

> **66** In order for the establishment to generate the maximum amount of business over the service period, with as high a net profit as possible, staff must develop a sense of urgency. **99**

Customer service and customer satisfaction

The correct approach to the customer is of the utmost importance. When it comes to keeping the customer happy you should always anticipate their needs and wishes, so a careful watch should be kept on customers at all times. Care should always be taken when dealing with difficult behaviour and you should never argue with customers – this will only aggravate the situation. All complaints should be referred to someone in authority.

The food and beverage staff must see that the guests have all they require and are completely satisfied. If there is a warm and friendly atmosphere in the food service area, and good team spirit among the waiting staff, the customer will be comfortable in their surroundings. Staff should have a pleasant manner and show courtesy and tact, an even temper and good humour.

TOP TIP!

Never argue with customers – this will only aggravate a situation.

You need to ensure you never show your displeasure, even during a difficult situation, and if you are unable to resolve a situation it should be referred immediately to a senior member of the team who will be able to calm the guest and put right any fault. Loss of time in dealing with complaints only makes the situation worse.

In conference and exhibition organising, the main customer is the person for whom you are organising the event (usually the person or company paying you), but this extends to keeping visitors to the event happy, ensuring they have a good experience and developing good relationships with contractors and suppliers so that everything runs efficiently and on target.

Teamwork

Above all, the staff should be able to work as part of a team within and between departments. You can show that you are a good team member by communicating effectively with others, getting involved in team activities at school (sport, music, drama, clubs and societies, Duke of Edinburgh's Awards, project groups, charity events), college or in your local community.

If you want a management role, try to take an active part in organising events and activities, so that you can feel what it's like to have to take responsibility and lead a project or team of people. Activities such as peer mentoring or being a school representative for your year shows your willingness to get involved and work with others.

TOP TIP!

If you want a management role, try to take an active part in organising events and activities.

The Association for Conferences and Events suggests gaining experience during the holiday period or during a gap year. Get involved in organising a garden fête, gymkhana, street procession or local charity event, or approach the National Trust or English Heritage to find out about cultural events in your own locality.

Literacy and numeracy

Most college courses and work-based training routes will include a procedure for assessing your levels of literacy and numeracy. These skills are fundamental to being able to cope with a modern lifestyle and with work in an increasingly technical and advanced society. If you don't do very well in your GCSEs, you might want to re-sit them, or work towards numeracy and literacy awards, while also moving ahead with a vocational course or training. If you are unsure, most education providers, and services such as Connexions, can offer information, advice and guidance related to the right learning support and where you can find this type of provision in your local area.

NEWSFLASH!

Venues are required by law to have a Phonographic Performance Ltd (PPL) licence for playing music in public. Studies have shown that the use of certain music can prompt customers to finish their meals quicker or to remain longer on the premises.

Computer literacy

Now required for most jobs, the way you use computers will depend on your specific job role. If you work in a reception area, you will need to learn how to use a computerised booking system. If you are a manager, you will need to purchase the most appropriate systems for your business, or multimedia equipment for hotel rooms, and understand the benefits of the technology on offer. You may need to understand computerised accounts, stocktaking and ordering systems, spreadsheets and/or to type business letters and reports effectively, or to enter data without errors.

Computer literacy is certainly required for events management, conference and exhibition organising, and some companies provide additional technical support, such as audiovisual equipment for events, so a basic knowledge of how to interpret customer needs in the context of new and diverse technologies is relevant and useful.

Business and management skills

If you want to progress to management, you will need excellent communication skills, both oral and written. You will also need the confidence to: make new business contacts to secure the continued development of the business; attend or chair meetings; be able to write reports, policies and procedures; budget effectively and maximise profits.

You may need to work long hours and develop lots of stamina as well as have the ability to plan for business success in the short, medium and long term. If you are self-employed, you may have to work out your own tax returns, forecast profits and complete detailed accounts.

You will also need the knowledge to compete in the industry and survive, perhaps not just in the UK market, but also internationally. So you will need to ensure that you and your staff adhere to regulations, and are properly trained and qualified.

> 66 In this industry, sales, operations and marketing skills are particularly useful in management roles. 99

Familiarise yourself with career structures within the industry you intend to manage: for example, exhibition organisers vary greatly in size, from one-person operations to huge multinational conglomerates, and career structures differ greatly between these companies. In this industry, sales, operations and marketing skills are particularly useful in management roles.

Foreign languages

As the hospitality and events sectors are heavily linked to tourism, and also because we live in a multicultural society and an increasingly global community, knowledge of foreign languages will be useful. French is especially useful if you are working in food and beverage services because many French terms are used, and some restaurants even print their menus in French.

It would be useful to have some spoken knowledge of the language concerned if you work in a restaurant specialising in a particular type of cuisine, or if you are working in a hotel reception, so that you can understand basic greetings and phrases you might come across when dealing with international guests.

These skills are also useful in events management and corporate hospitality.

CHAPTER 7
FAQs

By now, you should be aware of what it takes to work successfully in hospitality and event management, and realise that there are lots of varying career opportunities to explore. But what can you expect day to day? How would a career in this industry affect your lifestyle and your long-term plans?

This chapter answers some of the most frequently asked questions about the personal aspects of working in the industry. It should help you make up your mind whether you want to pursue some of the job ideas further.

Q 66 **What help and advice can I get if I want to set up my own business?** 99

A The Prince's Youth Business Trust can help young people get started in terms of business start-up loans, short courses on what to consider if you are setting up on your own or with a partner, advice on writing business plans, devising a marketing strategy, etc. Go to their website, listed in the final section, to find the office nearest your home town. Business Link can also offer advice, as can Learning Zone staff in some local colleges; and there are also Women into Business initiatives. Look out for competitions for young entrepreneurs in business or trade magazines or on industry websites. See your Connexions personal adviser for help and advice, and talk to other employers about how they started out. College courses in hospitality at NVQ level 3 or certainly at HNC/ HND or degree level will usually have some supervisory or business management modules to give you a good introduction.

Q 66 **Will I get time off for holidays?** 99

A Yes, of course. You must remember, though, that the peak holiday season is when you will be busiest in the hospitality industry, and you might have to take your holiday at other, quieter times. It might be cheaper then, though, which is a benefit! Many careers involve working shifts and often over weekends and at times when your friends and family might be free. All careers information for conference and events management emphasises that it is not a nine-to-five industry, and you can expect irregular hours. However, shift work, part-time, seasonal and temporary work, and time off in the week, offer you some flexibility too.

> 66 You must remember that the peak holiday season is when you will be busiest in the hospitality industry, and you might have to take your holiday at other, quieter times. 99

Q 66 **What opportunities are there to work overseas?** 99

A Having just read a job advertisement for a head waiter and also luxury spa manager in the Maldives, I would have to conclude that the opportunities for working abroad are pretty fantastic if you are flexible enough in your commitments, relationships and lifestyle to be able to up sticks and go to where the opportunities are.

> 66 If you feel ok about meeting new people and not being around family and friends for a while, then go for it! 99

There are job opportunities at all levels and in five-star international hotels. If you feel ok about meeting new people and not being around family and friends for a while, then go for it! There are also opportunities to work overseas in events and conference management, perhaps in corporate hospitality in an international hotel chain, or as part of an independent events company, perhaps eventually setting up your own business.

Opportunities for marketing company services via the internet and other new technologies have never been so accessible.

Q
A
66 Will I need to be able to drive? 99

It is an advantage if you are working awkward shifts and are concerned about getting public transport at inconvenient hours, perhaps having to pay a late night or Sunday supplement, etc. However, many hotels have an arrangement with a local taxi company to help staff and guests, and some hotels may allow you to stay overnight. Being mobile also means that you can look for jobs further away from home, perhaps in luxury hotels or restaurants out in the countryside. If you are a mobile independent caterer, of course, it's imperative that you have a van and a clean driving licence.

Q
A
66 How much can I expect to earn? 99

Salaries vary considerably, depending on the job role, your experience and position in the company. Starting salaries for trainee restaurant or catering managers can be between £16,000 and £20,000 a year, but with experience this could rise to around £35,000. Pay for an events assistant is around £16,000, but with experience, managers earn around £45,000.

Working behind a bar could earn you between £11,000 and £14,000, rising to approximately £17,000 with experience and supervisory responsibility. Tips from customers can increase earnings. A concierge might start on £12,000 per annum, but a head concierge in a four- or five-star establishment could earn up to £25,000 or more. Bakers can earn between £11,000 and £19,000 but with experience and specialist skills could earn between £25,000 and £30,000. A trainee (commis) chef may earn £12,000 but an executive head chef in a top hotel can earn between £40,000 and £50,000.

Remember that wherever you start in hospitality, there is always a training and study route that can take you further if you are motivated and impress those you work with.

Q 66 **Where can I find out more?** 99

A There is a list of useful addresses and websites in Chapter 11 of this book. Useful trade journals are *Caterer and Hotel Keeper* and *Discretion* magazine. Check the Springboard website for copies of *Careerscope*. Some of the journals may be pricey.

For events management, conference and exhibition organising, it is important to understand the industry by reading the trade press, knowing about venues and keeping up to date with what is going on. The following are two leading, monthly trade magazines that include vacancy listings.

- ▶ *Event*: published by Haymarket Business Publications. Some sections can be viewed online at www.eventmagazine.co.uk.
- ▶ *Exhibition News:* published by Mash Media.

Also keep up to date by checking the websites of the industry's professional bodies: the Association for Conferences and Events (ACE); and the Association of Exhibition Organisers (AEO).

You could also talk to people in the industry, and try to obtain a part-time job or go on work experience to find out about some of the pleasures and frustrations in the work. Do some voluntary work, organising food and drink or an event for charity, to understand what it feels like to take on this kind of responsibility.

TOP TIP!

For events management, conference and exhibition organising, it is important to understand the industry by reading the trade press, knowing about venues and keeping up to date with what is going on.

If you think you might enjoy being a chef, try out some cooking on the family, and when you attend a function such as a wedding, observe the amount of organisation involved, and the roles of the hospitality staff you see.

Next time you go on holiday, have a good look at those staff who do their best to make your stay a good one, and think about times when you don't experience good customer service, and how it feels. It's good to make contacts. Remember, many people find work through their own networks, so now is the time to begin developing yours!

Q 66 **How do I get started in events work as a school leaver?** 99

A Start recording all your activities, as this will help you build a curriculum vitae (CV) and form your 'selling points' for the future. Look for part-time or voluntary work in your local community. You will probably be starting in a sales environment and proving your worth as you work your way up. Even at junior marketing level, employers will probably be asking for 18 months' experience. A school leaver would be best advised to build up work experience and then look for a junior position in the exhibition industry. Work experience is useful at any stage and may be paid or unpaid. Unless arranged as part of school or college work experience, it may be up to you to approach companies and arrange your own placement. Just check in writing that you are covered by the company's public liability insurance in case of accident.

Timing is also crucial. If an employer receives an application or expression of interest a few weeks before a big show they may be glad of help. If you can demonstrate enthusiasm and motivation, this is possibly the best way to get your foot in the door. If you cannot find work experience in the exhibition industry,

> 66 Timing is crucial. If an employer receives an application or expression of interest a few weeks before a big show they may be glad of help. 99

the next best option is to obtain experience in a related industry, such as sales, marketing, promotion or publishing. Administration in any industry will strengthen your application to organisers or venues.

Also bear in mind that this is an industry that thrives on face-to-face interaction and networking. It may well be that you reap the biggest reward by visiting shows/events and speaking to those directly involved. For a complete show listing visit www.exhibitions. co.uk.

Q 66 **What do events organisers do day to day?** 99

A People involved in events management may have to sort out how to advertise and promote events through mail shots, radio or other media. They may need to find a suitable venue and then generate income by selling exhibition space or charging fees to attend. Finding a venue is only the beginning, as floor plans, printed materials and equipment hire also need to be sorted out. Insurance cover and other legal requirements, including licensing laws, security, parking and transport needs will have to be met.

There will be a lot of communication with relevant people, such as catering staff, accommodation providers, contractors and suppliers (e.g. marquee and staging), negotiation with sponsors and organising ticket sales.

> 66 Progressing in this kind of organisation requires the ability to prioritise, follow up on things and be persistent to achieve what is necessary. 99

Organisers keep track of finances and stay within budget. In addition, they may have to arrange a programme of speakers, demonstrations or workshops, depending on the event. Progressing in this kind of organisation requires the ability to prioritise, follow up on things and be persistent to achieve what is necessary. You should be able to anticipate risks and problems and have the answer ready, all the while remaining cheerful.

A colleague who organises classical music concerts once had to find a professional harpist at short notice, because another musician had fallen ill, and arrange transport from Scotland for a concert the following evening. Perhaps a personal motto would have to be 'Don't Panic'!

Another example of an organisational role where there are current job opportunities is that of housekeeping manager. You could work in a hotel in the UK or abroad, in a luxury health resort, a hospital, residential or nursing home, holiday centre, cruise liner, golf club or school.

Daily tasks involve planning work rotas and supervising the work of room attendants, cleaners, laundry and linen staff. You will be ordering and issuing cleaning materials, bedding and towels; checking equipment, furnishings, decorations, etc., and arranging repairs and maintenance.

> 66 The ability to multitask is pretty fundamental! 99

Competent administrative skills will be needed as you will be writing reports and completing paperwork, ensuring laws and regulations are observed by staff. In smaller establishments your duties may include some cleaning, so the ability to multitask is pretty fundamental!

If you are not the organisational sort, you might want to think about a role where you are more likely to be given instructions than have to think of them for yourself or for others. For examples of duties you might carry out in other job roles, see Chapter 4.

Q 66 I'm a creative person. How can I use my own ideas? 99

A There is lots of scope for using creativity in the hospitality and events industry. The route you choose will depend on how you want to use your creative skills. For example, as a chef you might design and cook your own fabulous menu or a particular meal that excites and draws in the public.

As a food photographer, you might help to compile a recipe book, market a new product or restaurant; as a graphic or web designer you could help to create digital images or interactive functions on a website to help a company market its services or an event. If you are creative with lighting and sound, your technical expertise may be needed at events such as concerts or music festivals.

If you are creative with words, you might work for a publishing, advertising or media company and become involved in events work, writing press releases or features about an event or place. If you are creative in terms of being able to think on your feet, come up with new ideas and solve problems, your talents might lie in management, public relations, marketing, consultancy, business development or setting up your own business.

> ❝ You will never be bored in this rapidly changing sector. ❞

You may have a flair for interior, stage or set design, or even floristry, so could help with transforming a venue. Perhaps you decorate cakes in your own time, and decide to develop this skill to provide cakes for special functions such as weddings, birthdays or anniversaries. You may be an inspirational trainer or just good at suggesting obvious ways to improve the customer experience. Certainly, you will never be bored in this rapidly changing sector.

 Q ❝ **Will I be able to progress quite quickly?** ❞

A That will depend on your abilities and what you want out of the job. More skilled workers will be needed in the lead-up to the 2012 Olympic Games. If you are ambitious and build up relevant skills, you can move on quite quickly. If you are highly motivated you could progress from an assistant to a supervisory role and on into management. If you want to, in most roles, you can study part-time while working.

Experience and the willingness to work hard have always been important factors in the hospitality industry, plus your ability as a team player and general communication skills. Sometimes it will help to have studied for relevant qualifications, depending on the role you're in and how competitive the job market is at the time.

> 66 Experience and the willingness to work hard have always been important factors in the hospitality industry. 99

Often, though, employers are looking for someone who will 'fit in' with the rest of the staff and the ethos of the organisation, so qualifications are certainly not an automatic passport to career progression. Prospects with small employers may be more limited, and people may have to move between employers to progress.

Once experienced, some people may choose to set up their own business, for example a restaurant, small hotel or events company.

In events management and exhibition organising, if you can consistently achieve results within set timescales (have you got that homework done yet?) and work well as part of a team you will quickly develop your career.

Q 66 **Would I be able to deal with awkward or difficult people?** 99

A If you read a self-help manual on how to do this, it might begin with the statement that there is no such thing as an awkward or difficult person, only awkward or difficult behaviour. This is hard to remember when someone is right in front of you complaining, and working with the public certainly has its challenges. In the hospitality and events industry, dealing with people and their behaviour is a large part of the job, as it is with many types of employment and life in general! In the case of a customer behaving rudely or complaining, it is important to know what your company policy is in this instance, and what the strategies are to deal with it.

This will form part of your training, and you will learn to try to detach yourself from a complaint, in order to focus on how the situation might be resolved to the customer's and to the organisation's satisfaction. Obviously, if the customer is particularly rude or abusive, or it is not within your job role to resolve the issue, you can call on your supervisor or manager for assistance.

It is important not to be rude to the customer in return, as this will give them further cause for complaint, and bursting into tears will not be helpful to yourself or anyone, even if you begin to feel 'put upon'.

Remember that you have been appointed because of your communication skills and this is your chance to use them calmly and efficiently. Try to end all interactions with a smile, and start afresh the next day, without dwelling on or worrying about 'incidents'. Difficult situations tend to remain in the memory, but they are usually in the minority, so try to focus on all the positives that have happened that day, and all the compliments and thanks you have received, as there will be many more of those!

Quick recap!

✓ Remember that wherever you start in hospitality, there is always a training and study route that can take you further if you are motivated and impress those you work with.

✓ Qualifications are certainly not an automatic passport to career progression.

✓ Many people find work through their own networks, so now is the time to begin developing yours!

CHAPTER 8
REAL LIVES 3

SHARON: HOTEL MANAGER/OWNER/CHEF

At the time Sharon and colleague Sue began thinking about a career in hospitality, they both had established, successful and secure jobs as teachers in a boarding school. Sharon taught physical education and Sue's specialism was music. Their respective children were going through the education system and the two women felt that they would like to take on a new career challenge, one which involved transferring the skills they had developed. They felt their real strengths lay in providing a service and in their enjoyment of working with people.

It was Sharon who had links with Cornwall, as she already owned a cottage in St Agnes, a village near Perranporth. The two friends saw St George's Country House Hotel in 2005, a little too soon for their initial plans.

'You see something that ticks all your boxes. You have to make your decision or be prepared to walk away and wait until the next thing comes along. We had to ask, "Are we really going to do it?" '

It was a huge decision, affecting not just their teaching jobs of over 20 years, but impacting on the lives of both families. However, they were used to commitment to a career.

'Teaching in the boarding school required being available from 7am to 6pm, and also weekends. It was all you thought about until the holidays', says Sharon.

They decided to go for it and gave up their teaching careers. Sharon decided to be the hotel chef (in addition to general management, which she shared with Sue). She had a home economics exam pass (Food Technology GCSE A–C equivalent), and remains self-taught. She also learned a lot from her mum, who also cooked. Sue's mum had run a bed and breakfast for years, so Sue knew what to expect, having grown up in a hospitality environment.

> 66 It's important that your expectations are realistic. It is hard work. 99

Sharon adds: 'It's important that your expectations are realistic. It is hard work. Surviving is our main achievement. We have turned a tired hotel around by ourselves. Everything we've done has evolved from our own ideas and hard work. No one else has made this happen. We were two greenhorns trying something new and now we have made the place look great and the quality of the product is also great.'

The hotel certainly has a homely feel, with all downstairs rooms (apart from the working kitchen) being available to guests. There is still evidence of Sue's musical interests – there is a piano and also guitars in one sitting room, and CDs are continuously playing softly in the background. Sharon's interest in sport developed with achievement in local surfing competitions. The hotel's success is evident from outstanding customer feedback written in the guests' logbook.

'We have been fully booked since the end of July, even during recession, says Sharon.'

The really amazing feature is that no other staff are employed in the hotel. Sharon and Sue take on a number of roles throughout the day. A typical day begins with preparation for breakfast, and then clearing afterwards. Then they enjoy a break, have coffee, reflect and plan. 'This is a really important time, as it's probably our only opportunity to talk, and look ahead to the rest of the day.'

Sharon then gets on with the laundry and Sue cleans and prepares the guest rooms. They usually finish by about 2.30pm, have a break, and then begin food preparation between 4pm and 5pm. When the hotel is busy, Sharon shops online. Vegetables are often provided from the hotel garden. Meat is delivered, but Sue goes out to hand pick the fish from a local supplier. 'I like to choose and handle it myself', she asserts. Sue then changes for front of house service, which involves preparing the restaurant, bar duty, taking food orders, preparing customer bills, etc. Work is full-on as guests arrive, often for drinks to begin with (Sue serves these from the bar, and helps with choices of wine for dinner). After their meals, guests are gently encouraged to have their last drink by 10pm so that everything can be put in order for the next day. Clearing up is usually complete by 11pm.

'When the hotel is fully booked, family members, who now live locally, help with bar work, waiting and rooms. The challenges are trying to say "yes" all the time, which is something we try to stick to as part of our ethos.'

The coastal walks around Cornwall are becoming increasingly popular, and Sharon helps with free pick-ups and drop-offs at the next point for walkers. 'It's good for business, as walkers will book in at the hotel and they are always hungry!'

> **❝** Finding a corporate image or identity was time-consuming, but well worth it. **❞**

When choosing a business partner, Sharon muses, 'You have to agree a philosophy – what you're hoping for. For example, we both wanted to provide home-sourced, local foods and supply a level of customer service that you don't see very often any more. Finding a corporate image or identity was time-consuming, but well worth it, because once it unfolded, everything else, such as our choice of interior design, followed. My advice is to have a plan, talk about it and make your goals achievable.'

The hotel is Sharon's home as well as a business, and she wants her guests to be part of this, hence the emphasis on 'home style'. Her interests now are travelling, grandchildren and exercise – walking, swimming and going to the gym. Although, she is quick to add, 'none of that happens in the summer'.

Future plans involve consolidating the business and maximising the hotel to its full potential, without it becoming too big and too busy, as it will be kept as a family concern. Sharon now believes that she and Sue have achieved the balanced lifestyle they sought.

'We work hard, but I think it's true to say that we play hard as well, reaping the benefits of the peak season in the "off" season.'

> **Sharon's top tip**
> **❝** My advice is to have a plan, talk about it and make your goals achievable. **❞**

CHAPTER 9
TRAINING AND QUALIFICATIONS

As we have seen in previous chapters, the need for the hospitality and events management sectors to invest in good quality staff training is vital for continued survival in a modern, competitive, technologically advanced society. Therefore, it is important to consider which method of training you will undertake to begin your career, but also to be prepared to continue training through taking part in continuous staff development as your career progresses.

No matter what vocational training you have completed in the past or how many GCSEs, A levels, diplomas or degrees you have, there is a route in. Below we will look at the various entry routes into hospitality or events, according to your particular situation. You should note that opportunities and requirements change frequently, so you must also contact some of the professional organisations listed in Chapter 11 or check up-to-date websites.

HOSPITALITY

Your options if you have no qualifications

Bar person

It is possible to become a bar person without formal qualifications, but you do need to be able to communicate effectively with customers, handle money or credit and debit cards and give the right change, and be able to remember or note down orders quickly. You also need to be able to re-stock the bar area and work quickly under pressure.

> 66 It is possible to become a bar person without formal qualifications, but you do need to be able to communicate effectively with customers. 99

Room/kitchen/fast-food assistant

The ability to follow instructions and communicate effectively are important for all these roles and if you are serving the public, the ability to remember orders or key them in electronically, handle money or payment cards, along with basic food preparation and hygiene, are useful skills to acquire.

Porter

To become a porter you do not need qualifications, but you do need to be polite and courteous at all times, and have a good knowledge of the locality in order to help guests. You could progress to other roles when you have gained experience, perhaps accompanied by part-time study, such as an NVQ in a particular occupational area.

Concierge

You do not need qualifications to become a concierge, but you need to be confident, articulate and well presented, with good local knowledge. A basic ability to speak one or more foreign languages may be useful. Previous experience of reception operations, particularly in four- or five-star hotels, is an advantage.

It is common to start working in hotels as a porter or receptionist or another front-of-house role and become a concierge after gaining some experience. Trainees may be able to work towards a variety of nationally recognised qualifications, including NVQs in hospitality at level 1 or multiskilled hospitality services at level 2.

Qualifications

Because people employed in hospitality tend to move around within the profession across different roles and occupations, this chapter will deal with just the main points of entry, relevant qualifications, training and progression opportunities. All information is correct at the time of writing, but it must be checked again before you enter the sector.

14–19 Diplomas

Students aged 14–19 years old can choose to study for up to 10 diploma subjects over two years. One of these is the Diploma in Hospitality. This gives students a well-rounded and varied learning experience.

Diploma in Hospitality

The hospitality diploma is available at three levels: Foundation (level 1); Higher (level 2); and Advanced/ Progression (level 3). Over the three levels you have the chance to study every aspect of the hospitality industry from food preparation and presentation to financial management, market research, customer service skills, team working and communications, and learning about the law and food regulations.

While studying all this you will also have the chance to take optional extra courses in a subject that could complement your course such as a GSCE in French or an A level in Economics or Business. You will also study core subjects (maths, English, science and IT), which means that your diploma can lead in any number of directions.

You could go straight into the hospitality sector and begin your career or you could go on to study a degree in hospitality or even business or events management. There's no reason why you couldn't choose a completely new subject or career direction once you have this qualification.

Apprenticeships

Apprenticeships in hospitality are available (after Year 11), sometimes with a local college, and with local training providers. These provide structured training (often for a couple of years) with an employer and pay at least £80 per week; £95 per week from August 2009. A recent survey found that the average wage for apprentices was £170 per week.

 NEWSFLASH!

Entry to Employment (e2e) can help to prepare those who are not yet ready for an apprenticeship.

In addition, Young Apprenticeships may be available for 14–16-year-olds. To find out more, contact the local Connexions service or visit www.apprenticeships.org.uk

Part-time study options

There are many types of vocational courses available, and at different entry levels, depending on your qualifications. Part-time courses are available that include a wide range of industry-recognised qualifications to improve the skills and knowledge of learners and enable them to embark on a career within the hospitality sector. Here are just a few examples.

Food and Drink Service NVQ level 2; Professional Cookery NVQ level 2

These courses can involve students working in a college restaurant, often open to the public. In this case, you would apply to the college to attend full time. The professional cookery course is suitable for those who wish to become chefs and is a qualification that will develop skills and techniques to enable learners to progress into a career in the hospitality industry. Learners will complete practical assessments in food preparation and cooking.

Alternatively, if you are employed, these courses can be studied on day release, perhaps as part of an Apprenticeship. You would apply to local training providers (details from Connexions), or direct to local employers who offer training opportunities. The training provider will usually be able to offer you assistance in finding a work placement where you will be assessed in practical sessions, and when competent this will be recorded in a Unit Record Portfolio. Underpinning knowledge is usually completed through end-of-unit tests or online assessments.

 **NEWSFLASH!**

NVQ courses can be studied once you have left school, but there is no upper age limit for entry to any type of course.

NVQ courses can be studied once you have left school, but there is no upper age limit for entry to any type of course. What does vary, and is often a major factor governing decisions about options, is the funding available. For example, you may/may not have to pay fees once you are over 19 years old for a full-time course, as this depends on college policy and government funding. If you are studying part time while working, your employer might pay.

NVQs can take anything from six months to two years to complete. It all depends on your level of competence, the effort you put in and how the training provider or college structures the course.

Top-up courses

Additional top-up courses are available at local colleges of further education for those working in the industry. The following courses would suit someone in employment wanting to build up their knowledge, perhaps in order to apply for a specialist role, or to add to their vocational qualifications.

Food Safety CIEH Award level 2
This course lasts two weeks and is designed for anyone working in a catering, manufacturing or retail setting where food is prepared, cooked and handled.

Healthier Food and Special Diets CIEH Award level 2
This is a qualification that, over the two weeks of the course, provides candidates with all the information they need to prepare nutritious food, develop healthy recipes and cater to a variety of dietary requirements.

Pastry Cooks and Patissiers ABC Diploma
This qualification lasts 34 weeks part time and aims to introduce learners to advanced principles, skills and techniques required by pastry chefs and patissiers who wish to enhance their skills and knowledge to improve their position in the catering industry.

WSET qualifications
WSET (Wine and Spirit Education Trust) qualifications are available at local colleges and cover all you need to know about wines and spirits. You would usually apply for this

kind of course if you are employed or self-employed as a publican or bartender, or manage or work in a licensed premises. You must be over 18 years old. They are usually short courses of a few weeks' duration.

⚡ NEWSFLASH!

The word 'hospitality' comes from the Latin word *hospes* (meaning 'guest' or 'stranger').

The WSET Foundation Certificate in Wines is an entry-level qualification providing a straightforward introduction to wine. It is ideal for boosting the confidence of new or inexperienced front-line staff in the hospitality and retail sectors. This course is often offered part time over about three weeks, and may be available in the evenings.

The Wine and Spirits WSET Intermediate Certificate lasts seven weeks and offers broad coverage of all product categories in the field of alcoholic drinks together with basic wine-tasting technique.

The level 3 Wine and Spirits WSET Advanced Certificate lasts 19 weeks and gives comprehensive coverage of wines and spirits, with an increased focus on tasting technique and on the application of the knowledge gained.

Personal Licence Holders' National Certificate
The BIIAB level 2 National Certificate for Personal Licence Holders is a nationally recognised qualification designed for anyone authorising the retail sale of alcohol in licensed premises. It lasts one week and is both QCA accredited and government approved, and has been specifically designed to meet the statutory requirements of the Licensing Act 2003.

⚡ NEWSFLASH!

Waiters can take part in special waiters' races, which are held as an annual tradition in different parts of the world. The events feature waiters running in their uniform and carrying items on a tray.

Full-time vocational options
Full-time vocational courses are available to potential students of any age, and are available at local colleges of further education. You might also like to check which vocational courses are available at your local sixth-form college or school sixth form. If you are currently at school you should apply early in Year 11 to guarantee a place at a college or sixth form.

After the age of 19, you will need to check with your local college whether you have to pay for the course or whether you can claim fee concessions. This may depend on previous qualifications, whether you are unemployed or in receipt of certain benefits. Check with your local college. There is no upper age limit on entry to full-time courses.

NVQ in Multi-Skilled Hospitality Services level 1
This is a one-year full-time course for students who have a keen interest in cookery and may be considering employment in the food service industry. The programme is suitable for a wide range of students in terms of age, ability and circumstances. There are no formal entry requirements, but you will have an interview and need to show an interest and commitment to the subject.

You will learn the theory to help you understand the practical elements of the course, which are food preparation and food service. The course consists of seven units for the full certificate, and may involve visits to hospitality events; there may also be a combination of college and work placement learning. Assessment is usually by observation of practical and classroom work and there are no exams. You will have the opportunity to develop communication and personal skills as well as your skills in literacy, numeracy and

IT. Food hygiene qualifications are also available, and from this course you can progress to level 2 or a Hospitality First Diploma level 2.

BTEC First Diploma in Hospitality level 2
This is a one-year course which introduces you to the hospitality industry and provides you with a good basis to either go on to a more advanced work-related qualification or enter the workplace. A BTEC First Diploma is equivalent to four GCSEs grades A*–C and is normally taken as a full-time course. To enter, you will normally need to have at least one of the following:

- ▶ a BTEC Foundation Certificate in a related subject
- ▶ a standard of literacy and numeracy supported by a general education equivalent to four GCSEs at grades D–G
- ▶ related work experience
- ▶ other related level 1 or 2 qualifications.

The course comprises six units, which are assessed and graded: exploring the hospitality industry; customer relations in hospitality; basic culinary skills; serving food and drink; planning and running a hospitality event; and safety in hospitality. Key skills in communication will be developed.

After the course, you can progress into a career in the hospitality industry, such as becoming a chef or receptionist, or in a variety of roles in the food and drink service and the licensing trade. If you want to carry on studying, you could progress to a more advanced course such as the BTEC National Diploma or Certificate in Hospitality Supervision. You will probably need to purchase a uniform and equipment for this course.

BTEC National Certificate/Diploma in Hospitality
The entry requirements for this two-year course are four GCSEs at grade C or above or a level 2 qualification in a related subject. This course will prepare you for a management position in the hospitality and catering industry and allows you to gain a basic food hygiene certificate. It covers the following areas: food and drink service; front office operations; accommodation operations; applied costing; personal selling; promotional skills; and European cuisine.

Another important part of the course is the opportunity to do a work placement in hospitality and catering establishments, giving you the chance to put what you have learned into practice. You also have the chance to go on educational trips to various locations. From this course you could progress to a Foundation degree in Hospitality Business Management or a career in the hospitality industry.

 NEWSFLASH!
The oldest private inn in England is still a popular pub today. The Trip to Jerusalem in Nottingham was established in 1189.

Professional Craft (Food and Drink Service) level 1 Diploma in Professional Cookery
For one year, you will develop your catering and hospitality skills in the same areas as level 2 but at a less advanced level. You can then go on to level 2.

Professional Craft (Food and Drink Service) level 2 Diploma in Professional Cookery
Another one-year course, this course is for people who have completed level 1 or for mature applicants with experience in the industry. You will perfect techniques in areas such as

full silver service, flambé, guéridon work, basic butchery, pastry work, supervisory skills and food preparation and cooking. A programme of visits is often included. You can progress to a level 3 course, such as the BTEC National Diploma.

Higher education-level courses

For those with A levels or an equivalent level 3 course, such as a BTEC National Diploma, plus supporting GCSEs, there are various courses available in universities and colleges, leading to Higher National Diplomas (HNDs), two years full time; Higher National Certificates (HNCs), often three years part time; and degrees in hospitality management and related subjects (three or sometimes four years if there are industrial placements).

Foundation degrees are also available – they take two years full time, longer if part time, and there are no set entry requirements. Degrees and HNDs normally lead to supervisory-level and management positions. You should check the entry requirements for each course by reading prospectuses or checking the UCAS website. Many employers will take graduates from a range of disciplines, not just specifically hospitality.

To find out where higher education courses are available, you could check the UCAS website (www.ucas.com) and you would usually apply via UCAS for a full-time higher education course. If in doubt, contact Connexions, or the advice and guidance staff/academic tutors from your local further education college. An example of an HNC/HND is given below.

BTEC HNC/HND in Hospitality Management
You will usually need A levels or an equivalent level 3 qualification to enter a Higher National Diploma (HND). If you have relevant industry experience, however, there is sometimes some flexibility on entry requirements for mature students. The Higher National Certificate (HNC) is the part-time equivalent. Units of study involve:

- the contemporary hospitality industry
- the developing manager
- customer service
- food and beverage operations
- rooms division operations
- management accounting for hospitality.

Specialist units might include conference and banqueting management, people management, food and society, and marketing, plus a unit on industry experience.

After the course, career directions might include hotel management, events organisation, restaurant and licensed trade management, or an honours degree in hospitality management or similar qualification.

A BTEC HND in Professional Cookery is also available for ambitious chefs, and there is a Foundation degree in Culinary Arts Management.

EVENTS MANAGEMENT, CONFERENCE AND EXHIBITION ORGANISING

There are no set entry requirements and no set promotion or career path into this growing area of work. Company directors can come from a sales background as readily as from a marketing background, and it is not necessary to start in a junior position in the operations department in order to become an operations director. No formal qualifications are required to enter the exhibition industry at present, and if you have a good general education you may be able to get started at assistant level and work your way up. However, relevant qualifications such as leisure management, business, sales and marketing are helpful.

There are at least 32 universities offering anything from two- to four-year courses in conference and/ or events organising or hospitality. Foundation degree, HNC/HND and degree courses are available in events management, or in events management combined with another subject, on a full-time, part-time and sandwich basis.

> 66 No formal qualifications are required to enter the exhibition industry at present, and if you have a good general education, you may be able to get started at assistant level and work your way up. 99

These courses include a year's work placement during either the second or third year, and students return for the final year having gained valuable business experience. Other relevant degrees are marketing, business, modern languages and public relations. Topics covered on higher education courses may include project management, events promotion, logistics, health and safety, planning and risk management. Business or secretarial qualifications are useful.

Foundation degrees usually take two years of full-time study. It is possible to take a Foundation degree at a college of further education and then top this up at a university. You will need to check which Foundation degrees are available in your area. Entry requirements for HND courses are usually one A level or the equivalent. For a degree course, you need a minimum of two A levels (or equivalent qualifications, such as a BTEC National, or Access course for mature entrants aged 21 or over), plus supporting GCSEs. For a complete and up-to-date list of higher education courses, visit www.ucas.com.

For those already in employment, the Association for Conferences and Events (ACE) and Association of Event Organisers (AEO) run short courses for those new to conference organising.

Relevant courses are also offered by CAM (Communications, Advertising and Marketing Education Foundation) and CIM (Chartered Institute of Marketing). There are part-time and distance learning programmes, and also NVQs in areas such as events, marketing and sales, which can be gained through assessment in the workplace. The learndirect website (www.learndirect.co.uk) is a useful source for locating other UK courses in exhibition/events management.

> 66 For those already in employment, the Association for Conferences and Events and Association of Event Organisers run short courses for those new to conference organising. 99

Creative Apprenticeships are also available, which allow you to learn on the job with an employer and gain qualifications at levels 2 and 3. Various specialist pathways are offered, including live events and promotion, and it is possible to become a member of a professional body (e.g. the ACE) and to participate in the training offered. Details of training courses can be found on the relevant websites for the ACE and AEO.

Industry prospects

The event/exhibition industry is a fast-growing industry and the number of people recruited is vast. Anyone who is bright and enthusiastic should be able to get in on the ground floor and not having a degree is not a barrier to entry. Most major firms recruit as and when vacancies arise, while smaller organisers and venues, which make up the majority of the industry, are usually looking for people who can hit the ground running. (Source: AEO website).

Experience can lead to the opportunity to organise bigger or higher-profile exhibitions and conferences, but it may be necessary to change employers to gain promotion. Some experienced organisers work on a freelance basis and there are also opportunities to work overseas. Pay for exhibition and conference organisers ranges from £15,000 to £50,000+, depending on the employer and the individual's role, experience and reputation.

For those interested in food science or food technology, a BTEC HNC/HND or degree is the norm in a subject such as food science, food studies or food technology.

To get on to a degree course you usually need five GCSEs (A–C) and two or three A levels, preferably in chemistry or biology. For a BTEC HNC/HND, entry requirements are usually one or two A levels or equivalent. You should check with course providers for the exact requirements for all courses. If you have a degree in an unrelated subject, you could improve your chances of employment by taking a postgraduate course in a subject such as food safety or food quality management.

Go to www.prospects.ac.uk for information on postgraduate study routes and employment opportunities, or visit the Institute of Food Science and Technology (IFST) careers website listed in Chapter 11 for more information. You could work for a range of organisations involved in researching and developing new products, including food manufacturers, retailers and supermarket chains, government research establishments, universities and local authorities.

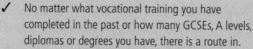

Quick recap!
✓ No matter what vocational training you have completed in the past or how many GCSEs, A levels, diplomas or degrees you have, there is a route in.
✓ Anyone who is bright and enthusiastic should be able to get in on the ground floor of events management; and not having a degree is not a barrier to entry.
✓ Be prepared to continue training through taking part in continuous staff development as your career progresses.

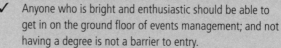

Access to hospitality, catering and events management

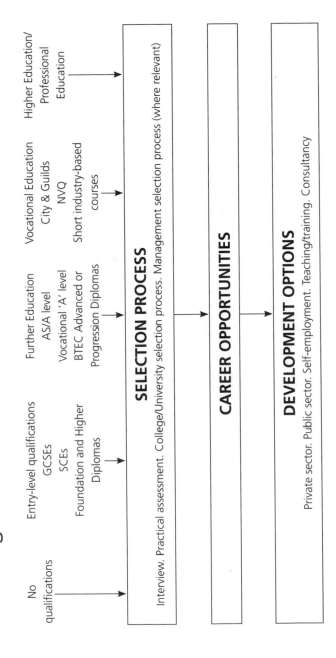

| No qualifications | Entry-level qualifications
GCSEs
SCEs
Foundation and Higher Diplomas | Further Education
AS/A level
Vocational 'A' level
BTEC Advanced or Progression Diplomas | Vocational Education
City & Guilds
NVQ
Short industry-based courses | Higher Education/
Professional Education |

SELECTION PROCESS
Interview. Practical assessment. College/University selection process. Management selection process (where relevant)

CAREER OPPORTUNITIES

DEVELOPMENT OPTIONS
Private sector. Public sector. Self-employment. Teaching/training. Consultancy

Career opportunities

MINIMAL EXPERIENCE AND QUALIFICATIONS

Bar staff, kitchen assistant, porter, sales assistant, trainee receptionist or administrative assistant, trainee chef or waiter, fast-food assistant, room attendant, cashier, banqueting staff

MORE EXPERIENCE/SPECIALIST EXPERIENCE/QUALIFICATIONS

Chef, housekeeper, conference and events assistant or PA, receptionist, wine waiter, pub manager, outside caterer, beauty therapist, hairdresser, lighting and sound technician, concierge, web designer, cake decorator, assistant catering manager, marketing and sales executive

FURTHER EXPERIENCE/TRAINING/ QUALIFICATIONS

Hotel manager, events manager, head waiter, banqueting manager, spa manager, operations manager, marketing and sales manager, restaurant manager, catering manager, reception manager, interior designer, consultant

CHAPTER 10
THE LAST WORD

You will now be aware that hospitality and events management is an industry that is fast moving and constantly changing and developing, as can be seen from exposure on television programmes and in newspaper supplements, tourism brochures, trade and other magazines. There is a tremendous range of jobs, from chefs preparing food, waiting and bar staff serving food and drink, to customer service for assisting guests and housekeeping; plus other interesting careers in events management, conference and exhibition organising.

> 66 Long-term employment prospects are healthy, but the hours can be hard and the work demanding. 99

You may want to work in food science and technology, become a butler, cake decorator or wedding planner. Or you might want to take up a traditional high-street trade such as butchery, fishmongery, bakery, confectionery, etc. Whatever you choose, there are great opportunities for progression both in employment and via a wide range of qualifications.

> 66 All jobs in this field require staff to be friendly and polite, enjoy good customer service, have stamina and be able to work well in a team. 99

All jobs in this field require staff to be friendly and polite, enjoy good customer service, have stamina and be able to work well in a team. Those in management positions must also have good organisational and problem-solving skills. Long-term employment prospects are healthy, but the hours can be hard and the work demanding. There are lots of ways in which you could gain employment and you could work for yourself, work part time or find work overseas.

Now it's time to do some of your own research, using some of the links in the final section, but first here's a small checklist to see if a career in hospitality or events is for you.

QUIZ

Are you prepared to work shifts or unsocial hours to get ahead?	☐ Yes	☐ No
Can you remain calm when confronted with demanding situations?	☐ Yes	☐ No
Are you an excellent communicator who enjoys meeting others?	☐ Yes	☐ No
Are you clean, smart, tidy and presentable?	☐ Yes	☐ No
Do you have lots of stamina?	☐ Yes	☐ No
Are you prepared to participate in training?	☐ Yes	☐ No
Do you enjoy helping other people?	☐ Yes	☐ No
Are you creative, or good at problem solving?	☐ Yes	☐ No

If you've answered 'yes' to these questions, congratulations! You've chosen the right career! If you've answered mainly 'no', you may need to re-think which career will be an appropriate choice for you. Think about what initially attracted you to working in the sector, and do some more careers research to find a good match with your preferences.

CHAPTER 11
FURTHER INFORMATION

There is so much to offer in the way of career opportunities in hospitality and events management that it is essential that you take a much closer look at your options than this guide has space for. In this section you will find a wealth of resources to help – websites, telephone numbers, addresses, and other books and publications. Have a look at as many as you can before making important decisions, no matter how much you think you already know. But there's no substitute for experience, paid or unpaid, so get out there and talk to people about their work so that you can relate what you read to first-hand accounts, based on real experiences in these fascinating industries.

Association of British Professional Conference Organisers (ABPCO)
Wellington Park, Belfast BT9 6DJ
Tel: 028 9038 7475
www.abpco.org

Association for Conferences and Events (ACE)
Riverside House, High Street, Huntingdon PE18 6SG
Tel: 01480 457595
www.aceinternational.org

Association of Event Organisers
119 High Street, Berkhamstead HP4 2DJ
Tel: 01442 285810
www.aeo.org.uk

Automatic Vending Association
1 Villiers Court, Upper Mulgrave Road, Cheam SM2 7AJ
Tel: 020 8661 1112
www.ava-vending.co.uk

British Hospitality Association
Queens House, 55–56 Lincoln's Inn Fields, London WC2A 3BH
Tel: 020 7404 7744
www.bha.org.uk

British Institute of Innkeeping (BII)
Wessex House, 80 Park Street, Camberley GU15 3PT
Tel: 01276 684449
www.bii.org

British Soft Drinks Association
20–22 Stukeley Street, London WC2B 5LR
Tel: 020 7430 0356
www.britishsoftdrinks.com

Business Tourism Partnership
www.businesstourismpartnership.com

Chartered Institute of Environmental Health (CIEH)
Chadwick Court, 15 Hatfields, London SE1 8DJ
Tel: 020 7928 6006
www.cieh.org
Careers website: www.ehcareers.org

Chartered Institute of Marketing (CIM)
Moor Hall, Cookham, Maidenhead SL6 9QH

Tel: 01628 427500
www.cim.co.uk

City & Guilds
1 Giltspur Street, London EC1A 9DD
Tel: 020 7294 2800
www.cityandguilds.com

Developing Hospitality Ltd
96 Rodwell Avenue, Weymouth DT4 8SQ
Tel: 0845 170 0001
www.developinghospitality.co.uk

Education Development International (GOAL)
International House, Siskin Parkway East, Middlemarch
Business Park, Coventry CV3 4PE
Tel: 0870 720 2909
www.goalonline.co.uk

Eventia
5th Floor, Galbraith House, 141 Great Charles Street,
Birmingham B3 3LG
Tel: 0870 112 6970
www.eventia.org.uk

Federation of Bakers
6 Catherine Street, London WC2B 5JW
Tel: 020 7420 7190
www.bakersfederation.org.uk

Food Standards Agency
Aviation House, 125 Kingsway, London WC2B 6NH
Tel: 020 7276 8000
www.foodstandards.gov.uk

Guild of Professional English Butlers
PO Box 35, Hayling Island PO11 0ZN
Tel: 023 9263 7919
www.guildofbutlers.com

IFST Careers
www.foodtechcareers.org

Improve Ltd
(The Food and Drink Sector Skills Council)
Providence House, 2 Innovation Close, York YO10 5ZF
Tel: 0845 644 0448
www.improve-skills.co.uk
www.improveltd.co.uk

Institute of Food Science and Technology (IFST)
5 Cambridge Court, 201 Shepherd's Bush Road, London
W6 7NJ
Tel: 020 7603 6316
www.ifst.org.uk

Institute of Hospitality
Trinity Court, 34 West Street, Sutton SM1 1SH
Tel: 020 8661 4900
www.instituteofhospitality.org

International Guild of Professional Butlers
www.butlersguild.com

Learndirect
www.learndirect.co.uk

Local Government Careers
www.lgcareers.com

Meat Training Council
PO Box 141, Winterhill House, Snowdon Drive, Milton
Keynes MK6 1YY
Tel: 01908 231062
www.meattraining.org.uk

National Association of Professional Wedding Services (NAPWS)
Tel: 020 8090 1921
www.theweddingassociation.co.uk

National Skills Academy for Hospitality
www.excellencefound.co.uk

People 1st
2nd Floor, Armstrong House, 38 Market Square, Uxbridge
UBB 1LH
Tel: 0870 060 2550
www.people1st.co.uk
Careers information: www.uksp.co.uk

Royal Society for Public Health (RSPH)
3rd Floor, Market Towers, 1 Nine Elms Lane, London
SW8 5NG
Tel: 020 3177 1600
www.rsph.org.uk

Society of the Golden Keys
c/o Anthony Lynch, Hilton London Kensington, 179–199
Holland Park Avenue, London W11 4UL
www.goldenkeysconcierge.co.uk

Springboard UK Ltd
3 Denmark Street, London WC2H 8LP
Tel: 020 7497 8654
http://springboarduk.org.uk

Training and Development Agency for Schools
151 Buckingham Palace Road, London SW1W 9SZ
Teaching information line: 0845 6000 991

UK Alliance of Wedding Planners (UKAWP)
7 Churchfield Road, Coggleshall CO6 1QE
www.ukawp.com

UK Coursefinder
Tel: 020 7827 5800
www.ukcoursefinder.com

Wine and Spirit Educational Trust (WSET)
International Wine and Spirit Centre, 39–45 Bermondsey
Street, London SE1 3XF
Tel: 020 7089 3800
www.wset.co.uk

Worshipful Company of Butchers Guild
Butcher's Hall, 87 Bartholomew Close, London EC1A 7EB
Tel: 020 7600 4106
www.butchershall.com